IRRESISTIBLE

Invitation

RESPONDING TO THE
EXTRAVAGANT HEART OF GOD

PARTICIPANT'S WORKBOOK

IRRESISTIBLE INVITATION
RESPONDING TO THE EXTRAVAGANT HEART OF GOD
PARTICIPANT'S WORKBOOK

Copyright 2008 by Abingdon Press

All rights reserved.

This book is printed on acid-free, elemental-chlorine–free paper.

Original art, cover, and page design by Joey McNair

Participant's Workbook
ISBN: 978-0-687-64869-6

08 09 10 11 12 13 14 15 16 17   10 9 8 7 6 5 4 3 2 1

MANUFACTURED IN THE UNITED STATES OF AMERICA

CONTENTS

INTRODUCTION   V

WEEK 1: COMING HOME TO GOD   1

WEEK 2: A LOVE LIKE NO OTHER   11

WEEK 3: ALIVE IN CHRIST   21

WEEK 4: FIT FOR KINGDOM LIVING   29

WEEK 5: THE HOME OF GRACE   37

WEEK 6: PARTNERS IN THE GOSPEL   47

APPENDIX: FILL-IN-THE-BLANK ANSWER KEY   56

INTRODUCTION

Just picture it: a big, beautiful house on a hill. It's different than the rest in the neighborhood somehow, with beautiful gardens, spacious rooms, and all that you could possibly want—but more than you probably think you could ever afford.

Maybe you've heard about the gatherings that go on there, joyful occasions that draw people from far and wide. Maybe you've heard how guests were treated like kings and queens, and even though you'd been invited yourself, you never thought you'd fit in, so you didn't go.

Well, friend, another invitation has just arrived. How will you respond?

What that "house" represents is the fullness of relationship with God. It's not just about accepting him as your Lord and Savior. That's just the start. It's about the richness of a life lived with abundant grace, love, and communication with the very One who made you.

From the outside looking in, that house may appear too good to be true. But once you step inside, you'll discover an amazing truth: it feels just like home. This is, after all, the place you were made for, a daily existence that goes beyond just "getting by." It is a place of acceptance, of purpose, and of fulfillment—and the door is standing wide open.

Over the next six weeks, we'll be approaching that door together. Through questions, discussion, Scripture, and personal application, you'll have the opportunity to discover new truths about God and his extended hand toward you. It doesn't matter whether you're brand new at all this or you've been walking with the Lord a while;

there's always more to know. Keep in mind, though, that you'll get out of it what you put into it. If you're willing to wholeheartedly commit to prayer, study, and conversations with others about what you're learning, there's no telling the depths of transformation God can bring to your life.

STUDY FORMAT

This workbook is designed to be used in tandem with *Irresistible Invitation: Responding to the Extravagant Heart of God* by Maxie Dunnam. That text is grouped into six parts, with forty days' worth of personal readings and introspective questions. It is hoped that as you read through the book and work on the study, you'll take these questions seriously, reaching into the very corners of your heart with thoughtful consideration and prayer, asking God for his revelation and guidance.

If you'd like to take notes on what you discover along the way, you'll find journal pages at the beginning of each part of this workbook. These Insight/Application sections are to help you reflect on what you read and what God is revealing to you through this study. They are for your private observations; what you write down won't be shared with your small group.

This workbook is designed to be the compass for making sure you get everything out of each week's study that you possibly can. Keep it handy while you read the daily book chapters, bring it with you when you attend your weekly small-group session, and expect God to move as he ties it all together.

Here's how the six weeks will unfold. You will begin each small-group gathering with a short DVD message from Maxie Dunnam. Then you'll go over the main points of that week's chapter using a fill-in-the-blank format to initiate some preliminary discussion.

Dividing into smaller groups or pairs will then give you the opportunity to share on a more personal level. At the close of each meeting, we'll look at Scripture that will help us remember what we've learned.

During our six-week study, you'll notice that other activities in the church body will tie into the weekly subjects as well. That's because we are all in this together. No matter where we are in our walk with God, there's always more to learn, share, and receive.

Week One

COMING HOME TO GOD

INSIGHT

Use the space on these pages to record your personal reflections, thoughts, observations, or revelations that you discover while reading *Irresistible Invitation: Responding to the Extravagant Heart of God.*

APPLICATION

After recording your insight, consider how you might make positive changes in your life or way of thinking in response to what you have read.

This discipline will assist you in remembering and possibly sharing with your group or class some of the reflections that come to you during this forty-day journey.

DAY 1: INCANDESCENT AMAZEMENT

INSIGHT _____

_____

_____

_____

_____

APPLICATION _____

_____

_____

_____

_____

DAY 2: GOD'S CREATION IS GOOD

INSIGHT _____

_____

_____

_____

_____

APPLICATION _____

_____

_____

_____

_____

DAY 3: A GRACIOUS GOD

INSIGHT _____

_____

_____

_____

_____

APPLICATION _____

_____

_____

_____

_____

DAY 4: THE PICTURE OF GOD

INSIGHT _____

_____

_____

_____

_____

APPLICATION _____

_____

_____

_____

_____

DAY 5: COMING HOME

INSIGHT _____

_____

_____

_____

_____

APPLICATION _____

_____

_____

_____

_____

DAY 6: A ROADMAP FOR THE JOURNEY

INSIGHT _____

_____

_____

_____

_____

APPLICATION _____

_____

_____

_____

_____

DAY 7: TAKING IT ALL IN

INSIGHT _____

_____

_____

_____

_____

APPLICATION _____

_____

_____

_____

SMALL-GROUP MEETING

INTRODUCTION

Welcome—we're glad you're here. A place has been prepared just for you. Today marks a special occasion as we begin our group study of *Irresistible Invitation: Responding to the Extravagant Heart of God.* Your group leader will begin with a word of prayer, then we'll turn to this workbook's introduction and study format.

Ready to dig a little deeper? Let's watch a brief DVD message by Maxie Dunnam, author of the book.

POST-DVD DISCUSSION

We'll open our discussion time today with a few questions and statements from the DVD. Let's begin by filling in the blank for each statement, then we'll look a little closer at each concept.

1. For this small group to be effective, it must become a place where deepest truths can be shared with security and _____.

    ※ Why is it important that what is shared within this group stay within this group?

2. As we go through this study together, it's important that we regularly _____ for one another.

    ※ How can lifting other group members up to God make this study more meaningful for all?

3. Deeply rooted misconceptions of God (such as thinking of God as an angry judge or score-keeper) can prevent us from experiencing the full measure of _____ _____ in our everyday lives.

   ❈ Where do misconceptions of God come from?

4. _____ _____ _____
   is the best direction any of us can take.

   ❈ Why is it important for us to seek God, rather than just waiting for him to find us?

5. Above all, we must remember that God is _____; he is for us, not against us.

   ❈ How could a deep understanding of this truth affect a person's walk with God?

6. We must embrace this powerful understanding: God _____ _____. I am a unique, unrepeatable _____ of God.

   ❈ Where will this understanding take you?

PERSONAL APPLICATION

One of the most important parts of this small-group study is the opportunity for personal application. To make sure everyone has time to participate and respond, we'll break into small groups. Begin with the key discussion questions about this week's readings, and if there's still time after each person has had time to share, move on to the supplemental questions.

KEY QUESTIONS:

- ❋ What foundational ideas do you have about God? What life experiences or teachings have led to that belief?

- ❋ What things could stand in the way of a deeper relationship with God?

SUPPLEMENTAL QUESTIONS:

- ❋ Have you ever been amazed by God? How so?

- ❋ How could regular study of the Bible affect a person's relationship with God?

- ❋ What do you hope to get out of this study?

LOOKING AHEAD

During the next week, we'll take a closer look at the life of Jesus and what impact it has on our own lives. In the meantime, however, commit to memory the following verse so that what we've learned this week won't be forgotten.

> I have come that they may have life, and have it to the full.
>
> —John 10:10

Write the verse below:

_____

_____

_____

_____

_____

Week Two

A LOVE LIKE NO OTHER

DAY 8: THE HINT HALF GUESSED

INSIGHT _____

_____

_____

_____

_____

APPLICATION _____

_____

_____

_____

_____

DAY 9: WHY WE STILL PREACH THE CROSS

INSIGHT _____

_____

_____

_____

_____

APPLICATION _____

_____

_____

_____

_____

DAY 10: HE COMES AS HE CAME

INSIGHT _____

_____

_____

_____

_____

APPLICATION _____

_____

_____

_____

DAY 11: A LOVE LIKE NO OTHER

INSIGHT _____

_____

_____

_____

_____

APPLICATION _____

_____

_____

_____

DAY 12: THE STONE WAS ROLLED AWAY

INSIGHT _____

_____

_____

_____

_____

APPLICATION _____

_____

_____

_____

_____

DAY 13: THE GOSPEL BY WHICH
WE ARE SAVED

INSIGHT _____

_____

_____

_____

_____

APPLICATION _____

_____

_____

_____

_____

Day 14: To Live in Joy

Insight _____

_____

_____

_____

_____

Application _____

_____

_____

_____

SMALL-GROUP MEETING

INTRODUCTION

Hello and welcome! After your group opens in prayer, take a moment to write last week's Scripture verse on the lines below:

_____

_____

_____

_____

As we begin our second small-group meeting for *Irresistible Invitation: Responding to the Extravagant Heart of God,* here's something to ponder: how is Jesus portrayed in movies and on TV, and how is that different than what the Bible teaches? Does Jesus represent weakness or strength? Futility or hope? Compassion or judgmentalism? How we understand Christ will have a definite impact on our level of relationship with God.

With that in mind, let's continue with a brief DVD message by Maxie Dunnam, followed by a few questions.

POST-DVD DISCUSSION

Begin by filling in the blanks for each statement, then we'll look further at each concept.

1. If we are to truly know God and experience the joy of the kingdom, we must enter through the

_____.

   ❋ What does it mean to share in the death and Resurrection of Christ?

2. When God gives us new life, all of our
_____ are forgiven.

   ❈ Why is it important for our wrongs to be
   confessed and forgiven?

3. God is able to close the door to my _____.

   ❈ What does it mean to let go of the past?

4. Jesus is often presented as the _____,
caring tenderly for his sheep.

   ❈ What might be some characteristics of a
   good shepherd, and how might those
   apply to God?

5. The sheep follow the shepherd because they
have a _____ with him; they
recognize his _____.

   ❈ What's the difference between knowing
   God and knowing *about* him?

6. Just like the shepherd offers the sheep
_____, Jesus offers his followers
a place of provision, security, and rest.

   ❈ In what ways does God provide security
   or rest?

PERSONAL APPLICATION

Now it's time to break into small groups for discussion. Remember that each person should have a chance to participate and respond to the key questions first, and if time allows, the group can move on to the supplemental ones.

KEY QUESTIONS:

❀ Why was the death of Jesus necessary?

❀ What happens if we leave Jesus on the cross without considering his Resurrection?

SUPPLEMENTAL QUESTIONS:

❀ What does it mean to find yourself "not guilty," and how could an understanding of that truth affect your choices in life?

❀ What is the difference between optimism and hope?

❀ Is there anyone here who has not yet accepted Jesus as Lord and Savior, but would like to? (If so, please make the small group or Bible study leader aware.)

LOOKING AHEAD

Next week, we're going to dive into the concept of being alive in Christ. Before we do that, however, let's learn another Scripture verse to remind us of this week's riches.

> For it is by grace you have been saved, through faith—and this not from yourselves, it is the gift of God.

> —Eph. 2:8

Write the verse below:

_____

_____

_____

_____

_____

Week Three

ALIVE IN CHRIST

DAY 15: THE ESSENCE OF THE GOSPEL

INSIGHT

_____

_____

_____

_____

_____

APPLICATION

_____

_____

_____

_____

_____

DAY 16: ALIVE IN CHRIST

INSIGHT

_____

_____

_____

_____

_____

APPLICATION

_____

_____

_____

_____

DAY 17: CONSTANTLY ABIDING

INSIGHT _____

_____

_____

_____

_____

APPLICATION _____

_____

_____

_____

_____

DAY 18: HUMBLE AND AVAILABLE

INSIGHT _____

_____

_____

_____

_____

APPLICATION _____

_____

_____

_____

DAY 19: THE SHAPING POWER OF THE INDWELLING CHRIST

INSIGHT _____

_____

_____

_____

_____

APPLICATION _____

_____

_____

_____

_____

DAY 20: WHAT CHRIST HAS BEEN AND DONE FOR US

INSIGHT _____

_____

_____

_____

_____

APPLICATION _____

_____

_____

_____

_____

DAY 21: DYING AND RISING WITH CHRIST

INSIGHT _____

_____

_____

_____

_____

APPLICATION _____

_____

_____

_____

_____

SMALL-GROUP MEETING

INTRODUCTION

Welcome, welcome! Here we are at week three of *Irresistible Invitation: Responding to the Extravagant Heart of God.* After we open in prayer, let's recall last week's memory verse. Please take a moment to write it here:

_____

_____

_____

_____

Before we watch the DVD message from Maxie Dunnam, think of a very dark place and consider how much light a single candle can provide there. We can be that candle. No matter how dark things seem around us, the light that Christ puts in our hearts when we become fully alive in him can affect others far and wide. Let's watch together, then discuss the main themes.

POST-DVD DISCUSSION

As usual, we'll begin by filling in the blanks. Then we'll take it to the next step with some discussion.

1. The big word theologians use to describe the ongoing process of becoming a new creation in Christ is _____.

    ❋ Why is becoming new in Christ an ongoing process, rather than a one-time event?

2. The key to effective Christian living is accepting the _____ _____ as an indwelling, ever-present help and comfort.

❋ How do we access the power of the Holy
   Spirit in our lives?

3. Our calling as believers is to experience
   _____ lives.

   ❋ How can a life that has been transformed
      help others see Christ?

4. Jesus has a specific word of guidance for us:
   "Seek ye first the _____ of God."

   ❋ What does it mean to seek the kingdom?

5. The key to living each moment in Christ is
   seeking him in the _____ _____.

   ❋ Why might Jesus care about the details of
      our lives?

6. It is in daily interactions that we come to person-
   ally experience the common-sense _____
   of God.

   ❋ In what ways can we interact with God?

PERSONAL APPLICATION

Ready to get a little bit more personal? Let's go ahead
and break into small groups so that everyone has time to
share their answers to the key questions. If time permits,
feel free to move on to the supplemental questions.

KEY QUESTIONS:

❋ What does it mean to live a life full of grace?

❋ What are the characteristics of a person who is alive in Christ?

SUPPLEMENTAL QUESTIONS:

❋ How can a person be dependent on Jesus?

❋ Why is it important that Jesus was both fully God and fully human?

❋ What is the difference between being a servant and being a doormat?

LOOKING AHEAD

Can we really be halfway through the study? Next week, we'll tackle the idea of being fit for kingdom living. But let's introduce this week's Scripture first.

We are God's workmanship, created in Christ Jesus to do good works, which God prepared in advance for us to do.

—Eph. 2:10

Write the verse below:

_____

_____

_____

_____

_____

Week Four

FIT FOR KINGDOM LIVING

DAY 22: CHRIST FREES US AND FITS US

INSIGHT _____

_____

_____

_____

_____

APPLICATION _____

_____

_____

_____

_____

DAY 23: CLAIMING THE PROMISE

INSIGHT _____

_____

_____

_____

_____

APPLICATION _____

_____

_____

_____

_____

DAY 24: THE SUREST PATH OF ALL

INSIGHT _____

_____

_____

_____

_____

APPLICATION _____

_____

_____

_____

_____

DAY 25: THE HANDS AND FEET OF JESUS

INSIGHT _____

_____

_____

_____

_____

APPLICATION _____

_____

_____

_____

_____

DAY 26: COMMUNION THROUGH CONVERSATION

INSIGHT _____

_____

_____

_____

_____

APPLICATION _____

_____

_____

_____

_____

DAY 27: PLANTED BY THE WATER

INSIGHT _____

_____

_____

_____

_____

APPLICATION _____

_____

_____

_____

_____

DAY 28: CHOOSING TO BE WHOLE

INSIGHT _____

_____

_____

_____

_____

APPLICATION _____

_____

_____

_____

_____

SMALL-GROUP MEETING

INTRODUCTION

Let's begin this week's study of *Irresistible Invitation: Responding to the Extravagant Heart of God* with prayer.

As usual, it's time to review last week's Scripture. Have you memorized it? Take a moment to jot it down.

_____

_____

_____

_____

Here's something to think about before we watch the DVD message from Maxie Dunnam. Have you ever had something made specifically for you, something that fits exactly you and no one else? It seems like a decadent treat, but that's the way God "fits" us into our new lives with him. We are the only ones who can walk out all of the plans he has for us.

POST-DVD DISCUSSION

Let's begin by completing the questions below, then we'll move into deeper discussion of each one.

1. When we begin to fully understand God's extravagant love, we can't help but be

   _____.

   ❀ What could stand in the way of accepting such a great love?

2. The greatest challenge of the Christian faith is this: what Christ has been and done for us, we must _____ _____ _____ for others.

❋ Why is it important for us to extend the
reality of Jesus to others?

3. Jesus doesn't call us to do the work _____;
instead, he invites us to join him.

❋ In what ways can we join Jesus in his work?

4. When we read and _____ on the
Word of God, we expand our understanding of
God and how he works.

❋ Why is the Bible considered living and active?

5. Another way to discover God's will is through
Christian conferencing, also known as
_____.

❋ What does Jesus mean when he says that
where two or three are gathered in his
name, he will be there also?

6. Whether we're aware of it or not, we are all hard-
wired to hear God's inner _____,
through a "still, small voice," an intuition, or
even an audible voice.

❋ Why does God speak to different people
in different ways?

PERSONAL APPLICATION

Remember, it's important that everyone has the
opportunity to share thoughts and ideas. Let's divide into
our small groups so we can talk a few things out. If time
allows, move on to the supplemental questions.

KEY QUESTIONS:

❋ What does it mean to be free in Christ?

❋ Why do we, as a people, find it so hard to believe that God loves us as much as he does?

SUPPLEMENTAL QUESTIONS:

❋ Is the idea of being "crucified with Christ" uncomfortable or exciting to you? Why?

❋ Was there ever a time that you suffered that you knew God was with you? How did you know, and what effect did it have on the situation?

❋ What are the keys to an effective prayer life?

LOOKING AHEAD

Next up in our study of *Irresistible Invitation: Responding to the Extravagant Heart of God*, we'll consider the church as a home of grace. Let's bring this week to a close, however, with a new memory verse.

> I tell you the truth, anyone who has faith in me will do what I have been doing. He will do even greater things than these, because I am going to the Father.
>
> —John 14:12

Write the verse below:

_____

_____

_____

_____

_____

Week Five

THE HOME OF GRACE

DAY 29: THE DWELLING PLACE OF WONDER

INSIGHT _____

_____

_____

_____

_____

APPLICATION _____

_____

_____

_____

_____

DAY 30: THE BODY OF CHRIST

INSIGHT _____

_____

_____

_____

_____

APPLICATION _____

_____

_____

_____

_____

DAY 31: WHAT DEFINES CHRISTIAN COMMUNITY?

INSIGHT _____

_____

_____

_____

_____

APPLICATION _____

_____

_____

_____

_____

DAY 32: THE PEOPLE OF GOD

INSIGHT _____

_____

_____

_____

_____

APPLICATION _____

_____

_____

_____

_____

DAY 33: ESSENTIAL CHARACTERISTICS

INSIGHT _____

_____

_____

_____

_____

APPLICATION _____

_____

_____

_____

_____

DAY 34: THE PRIESTHOOD OF ALL BELIEVERS

INSIGHT _____

_____

_____

_____

_____

APPLICATION _____

_____

_____

_____

_____

DAY 35: A CHURCH SHAPED BY THE
GREAT COMMISSION

INSIGHT _____

_____

_____

_____

_____

APPLICATION _____

_____

_____

_____

_____

SMALL-GROUP MEETING

INTRODUCTION

Once again, welcome! We've got a lot to cover today, so let's open in prayer, then write the Scripture memory verse for this week.

_____

_____

_____

_____

Before we get to Maxie Dunnam's DVD, here's something worth some thought: the Bible teaches, in John 13:35, that others will know we are Christians by the love we have for each other. We're supposed to create such a wonderful community that others can't help but want to be part of it. How good at that do you think we are?

With that in mind, let's move on to the DVD, and follow that up with some discussion.

POST-DVD DISCUSSION

Let's begin by filling in the blanks for each statement, then we'll look a little closer at each concept.

1. As the Son of God, Jesus invited people out of their _____ _____ with his compelling, magnetic presence.

   ❋ Why was it important for Jesus to draw people out of their everyday experiences?

2. In order to be a home of grace, the church must cross _____ and take _____ on behalf of the gospel.

    ❈ What boundaries could potentially hold back a church?

3. Sharing, loving, and serving others might upset our usual _____.

    ❈ In what ways can we make ourselves more available to be used by God?

4. Sometimes the Holy Spirit causes discomfort within us through _____.

    ❈ What is the purpose of God's conviction in our lives?

5. When we ignore the voice of God, we miss opportunities to _____ others and be _____ in return.

    ❈ How might God instruct us to be involved in the lives of others?

6. When we take a leap of faith for Christ, he always meets us in the midst of our situation and offers his infinite supply of _____.

    ❈ Why is it important for us to take the leap before God will meet us there?

PERSONAL APPLICATION

We hope that, by now, this time of breaking into small groups has become a richly rewarding part of *Irresistible Invitation: Responding to the Extravagant Heart of God*. Ready to get to it this week? Remember to make sure each person has a chance to share before moving on to the supplemental questions.

KEY QUESTIONS:

* What do you think comes to mind when the average person in today's society hears the word "Christian"? Is it different than what the Scripture expects, and if so, how and why?

* How could a church that fully understands and lives out its role impact its members, its community, and its world?

SUPPLEMENTAL QUESTIONS:

* Why is it important to have a faith that's both public and private?

* What is the difference between the church as an institution and the church as an organism?

* What is the role of the Holy Spirit in a church that is alive?

LOOKING AHEAD

Next week, the final week of our study, we'll consider what it means to be partners in the gospel. First, though, let's introduce another Scripture to help us hold this week's lessons in our heart.

> Dear friends, let us love one another, for love comes from God.
>
> —1 John 4:7

Write the verse below:

_____

_____

_____

_____

_____

Week Six

PARTNERS IN THE GOSPEL

DAY 36: PRIVILEGED PARTAKERS IN THE PROMISE

INSIGHT _____

_____

_____

_____

_____

APPLICATION _____

_____

_____

_____

DAY 37: PRAYERS

INSIGHT _____

_____

_____

_____

_____

APPLICATION _____

_____

_____

_____

_____

DAY 38: PRESENCE

INSIGHT

_____

_____

_____

_____

APPLICATION _____

_____

_____

_____

_____

DAY 39: GIFTS

INSIGHT _____

_____

_____

_____

_____

APPLICATION _____

_____

_____

_____

_____

DAY 40: SERVICE

INSIGHT

_____

_____

_____

_____

_____

APPLICATION

_____

_____

_____

_____

_____

DAY 41: EPILOGUE

INSIGHT

_____

_____

_____

_____

_____

APPLICATION

_____

_____

_____

_____

SMALL-GROUP MEETING

INTRODUCTION

Well, here we are at the final week of our study of *Irresistible Invitation: Responding to the Extravagant Heart of God.* Let's treat this as a beginning rather than an ending as we step through the next door that God has for us. After we open in prayer, take time to share the memory verse with your group members. You can write it down here:

_____

_____

_____

_____

As we prepare to watch the final DVD message from Maxie Dunnam, consider this: without each instrument playing its part, there is no symphony. The conductor can't make music all alone. So why do so many of us expect the pastor to play all the parts in the music of the church? Could it be that it really is up to each one of us, individually? Let's hear what Maxie has to say.

POST-DVD DISCUSSION

Once again, let's fill in the blanks for each statement, then dive in for further study.

1. This study was designed to help build mental, emotional, and spiritual _____ between the God who loves us and our daily experience.

   ※ How can a better relationship with God lead to better relationships with those around us?

2. It's easy to know something on an intellectual level, but if we don't practice it, it becomes _____.

❁ What is the difference between knowing something in the mind and knowing it through experience?

3. The irresistible invitation to enter God's kingdom is about _____ and _____.

❁ How do we, as Christians, continue to practice our faith?

4. We have to _____ our _____; if we don't speak up and accept God's invitation, then we'll never know what it's like to truly experience him and his presence on a personal level.

❁ What are the responsibilities of being a Christian?

5. Now that we've read, prayed, and shared about growing into the fullness of _____ _____ _____, it's time to open the door to a new way of life.

❁ How can we show others what's different about God's love?

6. Will we live our lives in holy _____ from this day forward?

❀ How could the church's witness to the world be different if Christians walked in wholehearted devotion to God?

PERSONAL APPLICATION

It's time for our personal application. Let's break into our small groups and dig a little deeper. Don't forget that each person should have a chance to share their answers to the key questions before the group moves on to the supplemental ones.

KEY QUESTIONS:

❀ How can service to others translate to freedom for ourselves?

❀ Why does God talk more about money than any other subject in the Bible?

SUPPLEMENTAL QUESTIONS:

❀ Do you believe there are things that will not happen if we do not pray? Why or why not?

❀ Why does God want us to pray?

❀ What are some of the challenges we face in being Christ to others, and how can they be overcome?

LOOKING AHEAD

Here's a promise from Scripture to encourage you as you complete this journey. Let's commit it to memory now.

He who began a good work in you will carry it on to completion until the day of Christ Jesus.

—Phil. 1:6

Write the verse below:

_____

_____

_____

_____

_____

As we bring the study of *Irresistible Invitation: Responding to the Extravagant Heart of God* to a close, let's review the memory verses from each section. Keep these Scriptures close, and as you move into the next phase of your relationship with God, use them to help recall all you have learned in the past six weeks.

Blessings to you!

WEEK 1: COMING HOME TO GOD

_____

_____

_____

_____

WEEK 2: A LOVE LIKE NO OTHER

_____

_____

_____

_____

WEEK 3: ALIVE IN CHRIST

_____

_____

_____

_____

WEEK 4: FIT FOR KINGDOM LIVING

_____

_____

_____

_____

WEEK 5: THE HOME OF GRACE

_____

_____

_____

_____

WEEK 6: PARTNERS IN THE GOSPEL

_____

_____

_____

_____

APPENDIX
FILL-IN-THE-BLANK ANSWER KEY

WEEK 1
1. trust
2. pray
3. God's blessing
4. Passionately seeking God
5. good
6. loves me/miracle

WEEK 2
1. cross
2. sins
3. past
4. shepherd
5. relationship/voice
6. pasture

WEEK 3
1. sanctification
2. Holy Spirit
3. changed
4. kingdom
5. little things
6. presence

WEEK 4
1. overwhelmed
2. be and do
3. alone
4. meditate
5. fellowship
6. guidance

WEEK 5
1. comfort zones
2. boundaries/risks
3. routine
4. conviction
5. bless/blessed
6. grace

WEEK 6
1. bridges
2. meaningless
3. practice/action
4. do/part
5. God's extravagant love
6. recklessness